Vegetable Broth

Leftover Magic ....

Introduction

When I sat down to write this book, the US was heading into the second month of a government shutdown. The politics of this truly don't matter and are not relevant to this guide.

What matters is the fact that more than 800,000 government employees were working without a paycheck and 38 million Americans who get assistance to buy food were on the verge of no longer getting that money any longer.

While this has been a terrible experience for many people who have truly suffered, there's one bright spot. A huge portion of the population who was uninterested in stocking up on food or living a more frugal lifestyle have had a wakeup call.

More people than ever realize that things can change in just a moment and that they do not always have control over it.

This was just one incident that caused people to be concerned about food scarcity in their own homes.

There are many things that can happen which leave us without the ability to spend our usual grocery budget. A huge medical bill, an unexpected and pricey car repair, or a job loss can change everything fast.

But you still need to eat.

This book is about shopping for food with limited funds and still feeding your family tasty and nutritious meals. It assumes you have a bit of money to spend, but not a lot. At the same time, you might be living off the supplies in your pantry for similar reasons.

These recipes are not for folks counting grams of carbohydrates or for people who will eat nothing but organic food straight from the farmer's market. (Although, you can opt for organic versions of all the food mentioned if you're not in a bind financially.) If you're in an extreme situation, you're going to have to take extreme measures, and one of those measures is changing how you eat.

These recipes are simple, filling scratch-cooking to keep you nourished when times are tough. There are also instructions for the scratch cooking of some foods you may not regularly use.

I've given away hundreds of PDF copies of this book to people in need on my website, TheOrganicPrepper.com. And it was so popular that people asked if we could make a hard copy. So here we are, now in print form!

I hope the advice in this book helps if you're in a difficult situation. I've been there myself and I know it can happen to anyone.

Flat Broke Grocery Shopping

When your budget is super tight, grocery shopping is going to look a lot different. In my opinion, you're better off to shop for the entire month all at once when times are tough. Once-a-month shopping is a far less expensive way to purchase food, and I often do it myself even when things aren't too bad. For very in-depth shopping tips, check out my book The Prepper's Pantry, available in the spring of 2019 from Skyhorse Publishing.

Your Flat Broke diet

When you are doing a flat-broke, once-a-month shopping trip, your diet may look a little different than it normally does. Remember, your goal is to get through the month without going hungry, not to go organic paleo.

Don't plan on eating low-carb this month. Unless, of course, you have a health condition that requires a low carb diet, plan on adding more grains and starches to your diet during a rough spot.

Also, you probably won't be able to eat organic. If you normally eat nothing but fresh, organic goodness, this month is going to have to be different. If times are really, really tight, you are going to need to loosen your standards to survive. If you are rock bottom broke, you may have to go even cheaper.

So, when I recommend canned fruits and lots of potatoes here in a minute, I don't want to hear "But you're supposed to be the organic prepper." Sure. I am. But I'm also a sensible and realistic prepper. Just make the best choices you can while still staying fed, okay?

Let's go through our food groups really quickly to give you an idea what you'll be looking for on your shopping trip. None of these lists is comprehensive – you have to go with the things your family will eat and the things you can personally acquire inexpensively.

Protein

When you're broke, protein is going to be the costliest part of your menu.

Meat: When your budget is super tight, don't expect meat to be the main dish. I'm not saying you have to go vegetarian, but calorie for calorie, meat is very expensive. Use less meat than you normally would and make it an ingredient instead of the star of the meal. Go with less expensive cuts and cook them for a long time: stew beef, 70/30 ground beef, chicken quarters, chicken thighs, etc., are much less costly. You can also buy an inexpensive beef roast and an inexpensive whole chicken that will get you through several meals if carefully doled out.

Eggs: Eggs are a very inexpensive and healthy source of protein. Walmart has huge flats with 30 eggs for a very reasonable price. I suggest you grab a few of those and think about breakfast for dinner.

Beans: I absolutely love beans and strongly recommend them. Proper soaking and rinsing can reduce the resulting flatulence that a lot of folks worry about. Go with dried beans instead of canned for greater savings. (I'll show you how to cook them in the scratch cooking chapter.) If your family members don't like beans, they might prefer refried beans or bean dip. Worst case scenario, you can puree cooked beans and add them to a soup for a nutrient boost.

Peanut butter: Peanut butter is a tasty protein source and most kids love it. (Assuming there are no allergies, of course.) Grab a huge jar and if possible, go for one that is more natural. Skippy and Jif both have a natural peanut butter without a whole lot of additives.

Canned tuna: Beware of eating this stuff non-stop because of high levels of mercury, but some canned tuna will add much-needed protein to your menu.

Lentils and split peas: Both of these are high in protein, dirt cheap, and easy to turn into delicious soups.

Fruits and Vegetables

Produce is a very important part of a healthy diet. Without it, you're at risk for all sorts of deficiency diseases. When shopping once a month, plan to eat your fresh stuff early in the month and then move on to your frozen or canned goods.

Apples: If the price is reasonable, grab a large bag of apples. This will provide you with some fresh fruit.

Applesauce: This is a great addition for later in the month when the fresh stuff is gone. To save money, look for large jars of applesauce instead of the little individual packets for lunch boxes. Go with unsweetened applesauce.

Canned fruit: Get fruit canned in the lightest syrup possible, or fruit canned in juice. Just because you're broke doesn't mean you need to eat 10 pounds of sugar per day, right? Canned fruit is a nice addition to pancakes, waffles, or oatmeal. Reserve the juice for baking.

Overripe bananas: If your store has a last-day-of-sale bin for produce, you may be able to grab some overripe bananas. Get these and take them home for banana bread.

Carrots: I'm not talking about baby carrots here. I'm talking about those huge bags of grown-up carrots you'll need to peel and slice yourself. Remember earlier when I told you that you're either spending time or money? Carrots are a perfect example of that. Peel them, slice them, and keep them in a bowl of water in your fridge for yummy snacking.

Potatoes: A couple of bags of potatoes can get you through a rough time. Potatoes are filling, can be cooked in a lot of different ways, and most folks love them. Leave the peel on for added fiber. Store them in a cool, dark place away from onions for the longest life. Even when they're sprouting eyes, you can eat them though – just cut out the sprouting parts.

Onions: A big bag of onions will help you flavor up your home cooking this month.

Garlic: Sometimes it's cheaper to buy garlic already chopped up in a jar. Grab enough garlic to spice up your food over the course of the month.

Cabbage: Depending on the time of year, a few heads of cabbage will get you far for very little money. You can use cabbage in coleslaw, salads, soup, or casseroles. You don't need to get fancy – just go with the plain, ordinary green heads of cabbage if they're the cheapest.

Canned tomatoes: My favorite canned good is canned tomatoes. I like to get a variety of crushed and diced ones. These can be used for soups, chili, casseroles, and sauces. Canned tomatoes are a nutritional powerhouse.

Frozen vegetables: At my local grocery store, I can get bags of frozen vegetables for a dollar each, and sometimes less. If you have the freezer space, this is the way to go. I suggest you grab *at least* 30 bags of veggies that you know your family will enjoy. Our favorites are: peas and carrots, green peas, corn, cauliflower, broccoli, chopped spinach, Brussels sprouts, mixed vegetables, and green beans. With an assortment of frozen vegetables, you can make all sorts of great stuff.

Whatever is in season: Every season, there are fruits and veggies that are at their ripest and least expensive. What is in season depends on when your personal financial catastrophe occurs.

Dairy

If you consume dairy products on a daily basis, you're going to still want to consume dairy products when times are tough. (Cream for your coffee, milk for cereal, a beverage for the kiddos).

Generic milk by the gallon is your least expensive way to go for this. You can make all sorts of things from your gallons of milk, like homemade yogurt and cottage cheese. I suggest you put aside enough cash to be able to pick up a gallon of milk weekly. If you don't already have powdered milk, this isn't the time to buy it. It tends to be a lot more expensive than fresh milk.

Milk with lower fat can be frozen. Be sure to remove at least one cup of milk from your gallon jug to allow room for expansion. This works best with skim milk. Any milk with fat will need to be shaken each time you use it.

Grab cheese by the block for the least expensive option. Because we really enjoy cheese, I pick up 2 large blocks for a month. I cut each one in half and package them up separately. I freeze 3 and keep one in the fridge. Remember, cheese is *a condiment* during difficult times, not a main course. You simply cannot afford cheese and crackers for dinner.

Grains

I know this is a wildly unpopular ingredient these days, with all the low-carb and keto diets out there, but grains are the great stretchers of your pantry. You can take one serving of leftover chili and feed your entire family with it when you mix it with rice and a little bit of cheese.

Buy your grains in the biggest packages possible for the most savings. Forget about "instant" anything – these items are often totally stripped of nutrition, and again – you are spending time, or you are spending money. Here are some of the grains to look for:

- Brown rice
- Pasta
- Oats
- Quinoa
- Barley
- Flour
- Cornmeal

There are lots of other grains, but these are inexpensive, versatile, and easy to work with.

Basics

To turn your raw ingredients into meals, you'll need a few basics, too.

- Baking soda
- Baking powder
- Yeast (if you are going to bake bread)
- Spices
- Sugar, Syrup, Honey
- Fats (Cooking oil, shortening, butter, lard, etc.)
- Vinegar
- Salt and pepper

How much should you buy?

This is the tricky part. How much to buy has a lot of variables and only you can identify them.

- What do you have on hand?
- How big is your family?
- How hungry is your family?
- How picky is your family?

- How long do you expect the budget to be tight?

The best option is to do some meal planning before you go shopping. This should help you identify how much you need for main meals. Don't forget to add extra for lunches and snacks!

I know it's scary to face financial problems, but you *will* get through this.

At the end of this book, you'll find a shopping list with ingredients used in the recipes. There are no quantities given because this will vary by family and by how often you intend to use the individual recipes.

Where should you shop?

Remember, all grocery stores aren't created equally.

In every area, there's always a "cheap" store. It may be the one you don't usually shop at, but when you go there, you may end up with a much bigger cart full of groceries for the same money you were spending before.

I find that in my part of the world, Food Lion is a fraction of the price of Kroger, even with the sales and fuel discounts. When I lived on the west coast, Winco and Save Mart were the inexpensive ones. Walmart has inexpensive groceries in most areas.

Also check out places like Aldi's, Grocery Outlet, and Lidl. Some items that are name brand can be purchased at dollar stores and liquidation stores. Go to the least expensive place around for your shopping trip and you'll get more for your money.

Get things your family will eat.

A lot of folks with big mouths who have never been through what you're experiencing will give you ill-conceived advice like, "just eat ramen noodles" or "just eat beans and rice." They'll act as though you don't "deserve" tasty food just because you're currently broke.

If you embark on months of eating nothing but Top Ramen, you're going to be weak, lethargic, and more susceptible to illness. It's honestly a horrible idea. You do deserve nutritious things for yourself and your family and don't let anyone tell you otherwise. You aren't being punished. You're just being challenged.

It's important to get foods that your family will actually eat, too, because wasting food is a really bad idea during times like this. Making homemade, thrifty versions of their favorites is a great way to avoid waste. Obviously, if their favorites are steak and lobster, you're going to have to dial it down a notch. It'll go a lot smoother if the whole family works together and cooperates (which I know is easier said than done in these situations.

By letting your family know what's going on, you can help manage their expectations.

Scratch Cooking Basics

Lots of folks don't cook from scratch these days when it's so much easier to grab a can or a pouch. And because of this, many young people grow up without learning to make beans, rice, or baked goods.

Learning a few scratch cooking basics can really help you out when times are tight. Look at it this way — with just about anything you eat, either you're spending time or you're spending money to pay for someone else's time.

If your budget is super-tight, then you're going to need to spend time.

Cooking from scratch doesn't need to be difficult. You're not trying to compete with Julia Child. You're just making the simple basics Grandma would have cooked.

How to Cook Rice

When purchasing rice, brown rice is the best choice. It has more fiber and more nutrients than white rice.

Some folks avoid brown rice because they think it's difficult to cook. Take it off of the stovetop and cook it in the oven for absolutely perfect rice every time. For efficiency, bake your rice when you are cooking something else in the oven.

Ingredients

- 1 ½ cups of brown rice
- 2 ½ cups of water, broth, or stock
- 1 tbsp of butter or olive oil
- Salt, pepper, and herbs to taste

Directions

1. Preheat the oven to 400 degrees Fahrenheit.
2. On the stovetop, bring rice, liquid, seasonings, and fat to a boil in an oven-safe pot.

3. Immediately put the lid on it, remove it from the stovetop, and place it in the oven.
4. Bake for 1 hour. Do not remove the lid during the cooking time.
5. Fluff the rice with a fork and serve immediately.

Leftover rice can be refrigerated and used in a casserole or stir-fry. In fact, I suggest you make a HUGE batch of it to use in other recipes and meals throughout the week.

How to Cook Dried Beans

There are minor differences in soaking and cooking times with different types of beans, but if you follow these basic directions, you'll be successful. The obvious, common sense difference is that smaller beans require a shorter cooking time than larger beans.

Prepping the beans for cooking:

1. Start with one pound of dried beans. Our favorites are pinto beans and navy beans.

2. Pour them into a bowl and pick through them, discarding any beans that are dry and shriveled, and any little stones or twigs.
3. Using a large colander, rinse the beans well under running water.
4. Place your beans in a large stockpot. Cover them with water by 3-4 inches.
5. Turn the stove on high and bring the beans to a boil. Turn off the heat immediately, soak them, covered. You can soak them overnight, or a minimum of 4 hours.
6. Drain the beans using a colander, then rinse them well under running water.

Cooking directions:

1. Return the soaked beans to the stockpot.
2. Cover them with 6 cups of water per 2 cups of beans.
3. If you want, you can also add some meat at this point. Salt pork, ham, and bacon are popular choices. If you aren't using meat, add a tablespoon of vegetable oil. The fat not only adds

flavor but keeps the beans from foaming.

4. You can also add onions, garlic, and herbs to the beans now. Don't add anything acidic until they are fully cooked.

5. Bring the beans to a boil, then immediately reduce the heat to keep them at a simmer.

6. Stir occasionally to be sure the beans aren't sticking. The beans must always stay covered with water. You may need to add water during the cooking process.

7. Simmer for 2-3 hours. To test whether they are done, remove a bean from the pot and let it cool. Taste it – it should be tender, but not mushy. There are lots of variables that will affect how long they take to cook – weather conditions, altitude, and the age of the beans can affect cooking times.

8. When they're done, you can leave them in the cooking liquid or drain them, based on personal preferences. (I grew up down south, where my

family always enjoyed them in the "bean broth.")

Make beans in big batches so that you can use them in some of the other recipes in this book.

One-Pot Beans and Rice

Ingredients

- 1 cup of dried beans
- 6 cups of water
- 2 cups of brown rice

Seasoning options:

- Cumin, chili powder, garlic powder and onion powder
- Cajun seasoning mix
- Garlic, onion, thyme, and sage
- Bay leaf, tomato paste, and paprika

Directions

1. Rinse and sort through dried beans, discarding any that aren't good.
2. Soak the beans in the fridge overnight.

3. In the morning, drain the beans and rinse them. Then add them to your pot and bring them to a simmer for one hour.
4. Add the brown rice and seasonings into the pot and cook for 1 more hour.
5. Taste test to make sure both the beans and the rice are fully cooked and tender.

How to Make Gravy

There are two kinds of gravy, at least if you're from the South. This is how to make a simple brown gravy. White gravy gets its own recipe later in the book.

Ingredients

- 2 tbsp of meat drippings
- 3 tbsp of flour
- Salt and pepper to taste
- 2 cups of broth, drippings, or water

Directions

1. Add drippings to a saucepan and turn the heat on your stove to medium.
2. When the drippings are hot enough that a tiny bit of water splashed into the skillet off your fingertips sizzles on contact, use a whisk to mix in 2 tbsp of flour. Whisk vigorously until the flour and fat are completely incorporated with no lumps. You should end up with a smooth, creamy-looking mixture.
3. Stir in the water or broth. Broth gives a slightly richer flavor, but gravy made with water is still delicious and much more frugal. Using the whisk, mix the roué and water thoroughly.
4. Cook, whisking almost continuously, for 3-5 minutes until your gravy reaches a uniform consistency and the desired thickness. If it is too thick, whisk in more liquid, half a cup at a time.
5. Keep warm over the lowest heat your stove allows.

Gravy ROCKS because it can make a lesser cut of meat taste delicious. Your gravy leftovers (if you have any) can be used as the basis of a nice soup or stew.

How to Make Yogurt

Homemade yogurt is tangy enough to use in place of sour cream on potatoes or in recipes. Making it yourself is a fraction of the price of store-bought yogurt. You control the level of fat in your yogurt by the milk you choose. This will work with any type of dairy milk but will not work with non-dairy milk.

Ingredients:

- 2 cups of milk
- ½ cup of yogurt with active cultures (your starter)

Directions:

1. Heat the milk to 165-185 degrees F (use a candy thermometer – or, if you don't have one, wait until you are

starting to see some bubbles rising but the milk is not yet boiling).

2. Remove the milk from the heat and allow it to drop to 105-110 degrees F.

3. Meanwhile, put hot water in your thermos to warm it up.

4. Gently stir in the starter. You want it to be well-combined but don't use anything crazy like an immersion blender. Remember, the good bacteria that create the yogurt are alive, so don't kill them with too much heat or overly vigorous mixing. Just a whisk will do.

5. Pour the hot water out of the thermos.

6. Immediately place the mixture into the thermos that has been warmed with hot water and put the lid on.

7. Keep the thermos cozily wrapped in towels overnight (8-24 hours). It has to stay warm. When we lived in an

off-grid cabin, I tucked the wrapped thermos behind the woodstove at night to keep it at a warm enough temperature.

8. Get up and enjoy some delicious, rich, thick yogurt.

Tips:

- The longer you leave it, the thicker and more tart your yogurt will be. If you intend to use it in place of sour cream, leave it longer.
- Always save a little of your yogurt to be a starter for the next batch. I like to put a half cup in the fridge, stored separately so it doesn't accidentally get eaten.

Variations:

Flavor your homemade yogurt with sugar, honey, maple syrup, vanilla extract, fruit, or jam for a sweet sensation.

If you like it savory, drain it overnight in the refrigerator. Then flavor it with garlic powder, onion powder, and your favorite herbs and spices to use it as a spread or topping.

How to Make Cottage Cheese

Homemade cottage cheese is a tasty addition to several recipes. You can use it in place of store-bought ricotta cheese, too.

You can make this creamy deliciousness with only 3 simple ingredients:

Ingredients:

- 2-1/2 cups of 2% milk
- 1/4 cup of white vinegar
- dash of salt (optional - it's just for flavor)

Directions:

1. In a large saucepan bring the milk almost to a boil. As soon as bubbles begin to rise to the top, remove the saucepan from the heat.
2. Immediately stir in the white vinegar and the salt (if using). The milk will begin to curdle right away.

3. Allow the mixture to cool completely - about 1 hour at room temperature. (The longer you leave it to cool, the more curds you will have. You can even put it in the fridge overnight before draining.)
4. Using a mesh strainer, separate the curds and the whey. (Hints of Little Miss Muffet!).

The result will be a delicious, light and fluffy cottage cheese. This recipe falls just short of 1 cup of cottage cheese and just over a cup and a half of whey. If the flavor is a bit sour you can rinse the curds gently under running water, then drain again.

Don't throw out your whey!

Here are some uses for it:

- Substitute for water or milk in baking
- Use instead of water when cooking rice or pasta
- Use it for smoothies
- Use it in oatmeal or other porridge

Fry Bread

This is a great side when you don't feel like baking a loaf of yeast bread or dinner rolls.

Ingredients

- 1 ½ cups of flour
- 1 tsp of salt
- 1 tbsp of shortening
- ½ tbsp of baking powder
- ¾ cup of water
- Cooking oil or shortening for frying

Directions

Mix all the ingredients together with half a cup of the water and knead until you have a nice soft dough.

1. You may need to add extra water to get a nice dough.
2. Let it rise on the counter for 15 minutes.

3. Add cooking oil or shortening to a skillet and heat it up until it sizzles when you flick a drop of water on it.
4. Then, pull off small pieces of dough, roll them into little balls, and then flatten them into circles.
5. Drop them into the skillet and fry them for about 2-3 minutes per side.
6. Use a slotted spoon to transfer them to a plate lined with a paper towel.

Cornbread

This quick bread was a staple when I was growing up. My dad, who was a child of the Great Depression, loved nothing more than a big slice of cornbread topped with pinto beans in their own broth. Unless perhaps it was cornbread broken up into a glass of buttermilk and eaten with a spoon, a dish I never personally enjoyed.

Some people like their cornbread sweet, while others don't like the addition of any sugar or honey. This ingredient is entirely optional. This recipe is naturally gluten-free, so it doesn't rise much. If you want a fluffy cornbread, replace half of the cornmeal with flour. Maybe I'm a traditionalist, but in my humble opinion, cornbread is at its best when cooked in a cast iron skillet.

Ingredients:

- 2 cups of cornmeal
- 1 egg
- 1 tsp of salt
- 1 tsp of baking soda
- 2 tsp of baking powder
- 4 tbsp of butter or cooking oil + extra for greasing your skillet
- 1 ½ cups of milk
- 1 tbsp of white vinegar
- 4 tbsp of brown sugar or honey (optional)

Directions:

1. Preheat the oven to 400 degrees Fahrenheit.
2. In a bowl, mix white vinegar and milk and set it aside for at least 5 minutes to allow it to sour.
3. Grease the skillet well with oil or butter.

4. Meanwhile, in a large mixing bowl, combine all of the dry ingredients with a whisk, including sugar if you are using it.
5. Add eggs and honey (if you're using it) to the sour milk. Whisk until well-combined.
6. Stir the wet ingredients into the dry ingredients until they are just combined.
7. Pour this mixture into the cast iron skillet.
8. Bake the cornbread for about 20 minutes. The top should be golden brown and crispy, and a toothpick inserted in the middle should come out clean.

I used to make a skillet of cornbread for breakfast for my daughters. They'd eat it hot from the oven, dripping with butter. Sometimes, they'd add homemade jam or maple syrup. Leftovers can be wrapped in foil and heated in the oven, or microwaved for 45 seconds.

Variations:

Mexican cornbread: Add 1 cup of cooked corn, a couple of diced jalapenos, and a cup of shredded cheese to the batter. Reduce the sweetener by half.

Blueberry cornbread: Add one cup of fresh, frozen, or rehydrated blueberries to the cornbread batter. Sugar and honey should definitely be used when making blueberry cornbread.

How to Make a White Sauce

This is also called a "roux" and it's a thrifty and inexpensive basis for casseroles or anything that calls for a can of cream of whatever soup.

- 2 tbsp of butter
- 2 tbsp of flour
- 2 cups of milk (or one cup of milk and one cup of water)
- Salt, pepper, and appropriate seasonings

Directions

1. Melt the butter in a skillet, and then whisk in the flour.
2. Let it thicken up for a moment, then stir in half of the milk, whisking constantly.
3. Once this has thickened up, add the second cup of liquid and the seasonings.
4. Reduce the heat and stir every couple of minutes for five minutes.

Use your white sauce in your recipe or add some parmesan cheese and garlic to make a simple Alfredo sauce for pasta or rice.

Pie Crust

Pie crust isn't just for dessert. See the chapter Leftover Magic for savory ideas.

The beauty of my granny's pie crust recipe is the versatility - you can use what you have. Ideally, I use butter and water for the fat and liquid, however, I have used many different ingredients with excellent results.

This recipe makes enough for one double crust pie or two single crust pies.

Ingredients

- 3 cups of flour
- 1 cup of fat (butter, shortening, coconut oil, lard, vegetable oil)
- 2 tsp of salt
- ½ cup of liquid (water, milk, whey)

Directions

1. Place your liquid in a dish with a few pieces of ice, if available. Keep this in the refrigerator while you're combining the other ingredients.
2. Combine the flour and salt.
3. Cut the butter or fat into tiny pieces and incorporate it into the flour mixture, either with a pastry cutter, a food processor, or a couple of knives. Once the mixture resembles cottage cheese curds, you have combined it sufficiently.
4. Add your ice water to the mixture a couple of tablespoons at a time. This is where practice makes perfect - after you make this a couple of times, you will begin to know when it looks

and feels "right".   Use a fork to mix this into the dough - if you use your hands you will heat up the dough too much and the crust won't be as flaky.

5. You don't want to dough to be wet and sticky - you want it to be sort of stringy and lumpy. When you think you have the right consistency, squeeze some dough in your hand - if it stays into a nice firm ball, it's time to move on to the next step. If it is crumbly and doesn't stick together, you need more water.

6. Make the dough into 2 balls and press them down. Place them, covered, in the refrigerator for at least an hour.

7. On a floured surface, roll out the dough with a heavy rolling pin until it is thin but not broken. Fold your circle of dough into quarters and carefully move the dough over to your pie pan.

Bake as per your recipe's directions or at about 375F for approximately 45 minutes for a two-crust pie or 35 minutes for a one crust pie.

Pizza Dough

This isn't just for the best homemade pizza you've ever eaten. You can also use it to make homemade "hot pockets."

Ingredients

- 3 ½ cups of flour
- 1 cup of warm water
- 1 tbsp of sugar
- 2 1/4 tsp of active dry yeast
- 3 tbsp of olive oil
- 1 tsp salt

Directions

1. Stir water, sugar and yeast together and allow it to sit for 5 minutes.
2. Add olive oil and salt, then stir in the flour until well blended.
3. Knead the dough for about 5 minutes, then let it rise, covered, for 30 minutes.
4. Preheat the oven to 425F.

To Make Pizza

1. Knead the dough again, then roll it out and place it on your pizza pan.
2. Add your toppings.
3. Bake the pizza at 425 for 20-25 minutes until the crust is done and the cheese is melted.

To Make Pockets:

1. Knead the dough again, then break off balls of dough. Roll them out and cover one half with the desired topping.
2. Fold the other half over the topping, moisten edges with water, and press them together with the tines of a fork.
3. Place the pocket on a greased baking sheet.
4. Once all the pockets are on the baking sheet, brush them lightly with olive oil. If desired season the top with a sprinkle of garlic powder and salt, or whatever herbs are appropriate.
5. Bake for 20-25 minutes, or until lightly golden brown.

Multi-Purpose Biscuit Dough

This recipe can be used for biscuits - simply bake for 10-15 minutes.

As well, you can roll this dough out and cut it into thin strips, dropping it into boiling broth until it floats to the top (7-10 minutes) to make dumplings.

Ingredients

- 2 cups of flour
- 3 tsp of baking powder
- 1 tsp of salt
- 1 tsp of sugar
- 1/2 cup of milk
- 1 tbsp of white vinegar
- 3 tbsp of cooking oil

Directions

1. Preheat oven to 425°F.
2. Mix milk and vinegar in a small bowl and allow it to sit for about 5 minutes.

3. Mix flour, baking powder, sugar and salt in a bowl. Add milk and vinegar mixture, and oil.
4. Stir just enough to hold dough together.
5. Knead lightly about 10 times on a well-floured surface.
6. Pat or roll dough about 1/2-inch thick.
7. You can move the dough in one piece over to your pie pan or you can cut circles with a floured drinking glass and place the individual biscuits on the dish you are topping.
8. Bake for 15-20 minutes or until golden brown. Top with butter if desired.

Vegetable Broth

If you ever wanted to make free food, vegetable broth is going to be one of your favorite things.

Directions

1. Every time you cut up or peel vegetables, save your scraps and toss

them into a tub in the freezer. Things like celery leaves and bottoms, onion scraps, garlic scraps, carrot peel, bell pepper centers – whatever extra bits and pieces you have, chuck them into the tub.

2. Once you have 2-3 cups of peels and scraps, empty the tub into a large stockpot with 8-10 cups of water.
3. Add some seasonings: salt, pepper, extra garlic, celery seed, extra onion, bay leaf, oregano, basil – whatever seasonings you enjoy.
4. Simmer on low for 6-8 hours. (You can also do this in a crockpot.)
5. Use a colander to strain out all of your now-soggy bits and pieces.
6. Your delicious (and basically FREE) vegetable broth can now be frozen or canned in 2-cup servings to be used later as the base for soups or the flavor for rice and pasta.

Leftover Magic

In these times of tight money and ever-increasing expenses, we can't afford to let anything go to waste.

One way to stretch your food budget is with the humble leftover.

Have you ever been really poor? I don't mean "I can't afford Starbucks until my next paycheck" poor. I mean "Should I buy food or pay the electric bill before the power gets shut off" poor.

I have absolutely been that poor, back when my oldest daughter was a baby. When you are that broke, every single bite of food in the house counts. You cannot afford to let anything go to waste.

This is where the "Ménage a Leftover" bucket in the freezer comes in.

Ménage a Leftover

In our freezer, we kept an ice cream tub. After each meal, those tiny amounts of food that don't add up to a full serving got popped into the bucket. And because of our situation, I often would take food that was uneaten on a family member's plate to add into the bucket. Desperate times, desperate measures. What people might consider "gross" in good times, they would feel lucky to have in bad times. Then, usually about once per week, the contents of that bucket in the freezer were turned into a meal.

I drew some criticism from friends and relatives during that time for the distance I went not to waste a single bite of food. A few people commented that it was ridiculous, others thought combining all those different foods in the freezer was "disgusting." and one person even referred to the meals as "garbage disposal meals".

 It stung a little at the time, but looking back, I'm glad to have had that experience. I can draw upon it if times become difficult in the future. While other people are trying to figure out where their next meal is coming from, I *know* that I can take the same amount of groceries and make at least 2 more meals out of them.

Free food!

I always considered meals from the leftover bucket to be "free food" because they were items that you'd normally throw out. So, let's say, you have a little bit of broccoli, some mashed potatoes, some beef gravy, a scoop of ground beef, some corn...you know? The remains of meals. What can you do with that?

This is where being creative with the spices comes in. I might take the above, add a can of beans and a tin of tomato paste, and turn it into a chili-flavored soup. Alternatively, I could stir in some yogurt and some noodles and make it into a creamy casserole, well-seasoned with thyme. I could sprinkle a bit of cheese on it, wrap it in pie crust and make turnovers. The trick is to make something totally new and different from it so that it doesn't even seem like leftovers.

Some of the concoctions were absolutely delicious - so good that we recreated them with fresh ingredients later on. Others were not-so-great. Only a couple of times did we end up with something that was really so awful we couldn't manage to eat it.

If you can serve your family one "freebie" meal per week that results in a savings, for a family of 4, of about $10 - $520 over the course of a year. It doesn't sound like much until you add it up, does it?

We don't always do the leftover bucket these days because times are not as tight as they were back then. However, we do creatively use our leftovers. Here are a few ways to remake leftovers into something new and delicious.

Leftover Buffet

We have some nice little oven safe dishes that are divided. We use these on "Leftover Buffet Night."

Simply put, all the items from the fridge are placed on the counter. Everyone takes their divided dish and helps themselves to whatever leftovers they'd like for dinner. The dish is then placed in the oven and heated up - sort of like a "TV Dinner" of choice.

Aside from the kids scrapping it out over the last enchilada, this is generally very successful. If you use a microwave, you can just dish things out onto a microwave-safe plate and nuke each meal individually.

Leftover Soup

When I don't have quite enough to make 2 full servings, but it's a bit more than one serving, I often make soup. I can broth on a regular basis, so it's an easy thing to grab a jar of broth, chop up the meat and add some vegetables and a grain. You can also purchase broth at the store in cans or cartons so that you always have it on hand.

You can stretch your soup by adding barley, pasta or rice. If you have fresh bread to serve with it and a little sprinkle of parmesan or cheddar for the top, you have a hot, comforting meal for pennies.

Cream of Leftover Soup

I use this technique quite often with leftover root veggies. Using a food processor, puree potatoes, carrots, turnips, parsnips or other root vegetables.

You can add milk, broth, or even water to thin the puree to the consistency of soup. Season with garlic powder, onion powder and other appropriate spices, and garnish with a tiny amount of bacon, chives, cheese or sour cream.

Other vegetables that are suited for puree are cauliflower, broccoli, and squash.

Leftover Pie

This is a great way to use up leftover meat and gravy. In the bottom of a pie pan or cast-iron skillet, stir meat that has been cut into bite-sized pieces with gravy. If you don't have leftover gravy, a creamy soup, a bechamel sauce, or a thickened broth will work. Add in complimentary vegetables, also in bite sized pieces. We like peas, corn, and carrots with poultry, and green beans, carrots, and potatoes with beef. Add seasoning if needed.

Top your pie with either a standard pie crust, cornbread batter, or with a biscuit dough topping. (Find the recipes in the Scratch Basics chapter. Bake as directed, then allow to cool for about 5 minutes before serving.

For even smaller amounts of leftovers (or picky eaters) you can use individual sized ovenproof containers or ramekins to make single serving "pies". I've also used muffin tins designed for the jumbo muffins to make individual pies. When using a muffin tin, you will want to make it a two-crust pie to enclose the filling.

Leftover Hot Pockets

If I bake it in a pocket, my kids will eat it. Whether the filling is savory or sweet, there's something about a piping hot turnover that makes anything delicious.

The key with a pocket is that the filling cannot be too runny. So, for a savory pocket, you can mix a small amount of gravy, tomato sauce, or cheese sauce with your meat and/or veggies, but you don't want it to ooze all over the place as soon as someone takes a bite. If you want to eat this as a handheld food, allow it to cool for at least 15 minutes before eating it.

You can use pie crust or pizza dough for your pockets. Pizza dough is our personal favorite because it is a bit more filling. I make pockets and keep them in the freezer. I take them out the night before and place them in the refrigerator. By noon the pocket is thawed and makes a delicious lunch-box treat at school.

We like pockets with veggies and cheese sauce; meat, mushrooms and gravy; meat and BBQ sauce; pizza toppings, marinara and cheese; and meat and cheese. Another favorite is empanada style: meat flavored with Mexican spices, mixed with salsa, beans and cheese. As well, you can fill pockets with chopped fruit that is topped with either cream cheese or syrup for a dessert-style turnover.

Leftover Casseroles

The fact is, you can mix nearly anything with a creamy sauce and top it with a crispy topping and you have a tasty down-home casserole. See the Casserole Formula for details.

Try barley, quinoa, rice, pasta or wheatberries to stretch your casserole. Instant comfort! For toppings, you can use stale bread that has been finely chopped in the food processor, cheese, crumbled crackers, crumbled cereal, or wheat germ, just to name a few items.

I often use things that have perhaps become a bit stale - just another way to use up a food that would otherwise be discarded.

Be creative!

You're only limited by your imagination when it comes to turning your leftovers into delicious, tasty new meals. Think about your family's favorite dishes. For us, it is anything in a pocket, pot pies and creamy soups. So, when repurposing my leftovers, I try to frequently gear the meals towards those types of foods. A hint of familiarity makes the meal more easily accepted by those you are feeding.

When reading the following recipes, think about ways to use up your leftovers that your family will enjoy.

Beans, Beans, Good for Your Heart

Every week, I suggest you make a giant batch of beans. (See Scratch Cooking Basics for instructions.) If you do not have pre-cooked beans for whatever reason, canned beans may be substituted. But home-cooked beans are *pennies*, so I really suggest you use those instead.

My family loves pinto beans, but you can use black, kidney, cannellini, or navy as you prefer. In this section, you'll find some easy recipes for using up your precooked beans.

Refried beans

Refried beans are oh-so-easy, and you don't actually have to "refry" them – or even fry them at all.

Ingredients:

- 2 cups of cooked beans (pinto, black, and kidney are best for this)

- ½ cup of bean cooking liquid
- 2 teaspoons of cumin
- 1 teaspoon of chili powder
- 1 teaspoon of onion powder
- 1 teaspoon of garlic powder
- Salt and pepper to taste
- Optional: 1 tablespoon of lard or cooking oil
- Optional: Shredded cheese and hot sauce

Directions:

1. Place your cooked beans and the liquid into a large pot.
2. Use a potato masher to get them to the texture you desire. I like my refried beans to be sort of lumpy. If you want a smooth texture, you can puree them in a food processor in batches.
3. Start warming up your beans on low heat, then stir in your spices: cumin, chili powder, onion powder, garlic powder, salt, and pepper.

4. Add your lard or cooking oil if you're using it.
5. Bring your beans to a simmer for 5 minutes.
6. Serve while hot. You can top them with shredded cheese and hot sauce if desired.

Variations

You can do all sorts of tasty stuff with refried beans:

- Make bean burritos.
- Serve as a side dish with a Mexican meal.
- Serve with Mexican spiced rice.
- Use it as dip with tortilla chips.
- Add it to beef burritos to reduce the amount of beef needed.

You get the idea, right?

White Bean Dip

Ingredients

- 1 cup of cooked white beans (navy, white kidney, cannellini)

- 1 tbsp of minced garlic
- ¼ cup of white onion
- ¼ cup of olive oil
- 2 tbsp of lemon juice
- 1 tsp each of oregano, basil, and parsley
- Salt and pepper to taste

Directions

1. If you have a food processor, it's ideal for this. Otherwise, you can use a blender or even a potato masher.
2. Puree together the beans, garlic, onion, olive oil, and lemon juice until the mixture is smooth.
3. Add the spices and run the food processor for just long enough to mix them through.
4. Let the dip sit in the fridge for at least half an hour to allow the flavors to blend.

This is tasty served with pita bread or fry bread. You can also spread a tortilla with the dip and add any veggies you have for a tasty lunch wrap.

Pasta Fagioli

This delicious soup gets better every time you reheat it. Also, FYI, it's pronounced fah-zool'.

Ingredients

- 2 cups of cooked white kidney or cannellini beans
- ½ cup of diced carrot
- 28-ounce can of crushed or diced tomatoes
- 4 cups of broth
- 3 tbsp minced garlic
- ½ cup finely diced onion
- 1 tablespoon of olive oil
- 1 bag of frozen spinach
- 1 bay leaf
- 1 tsp of oregano
- ½ pound of macaroni or other small pasta

Directions

1. Remove a half cup of the white beans and set them aside.

2. Add the rest of the beans, the carrot, the tomato products, the broth, and the spices to a stockpot.
3. Simmer for 30 minutes.
4. Meanwhile, mash or puree the rest of the beans with some water to make a thick paste.
5. Add the pasta to the soup and cook for another 10 minutes, stirring several times.
6. Add the spinach and your white bean mash and stir it in well, then cook for 3-5 more minutes.
7. Remove the bay leaf before serving.

Serving Suggestion

Top your piping hot soup with Parmesan cheese and a drizzle of olive oil if you have it. Serve with bread.

Chili with Meat

Cook this all day in the crockpot for a delicious, home-cooked meal with very little effort. If you do not have a crockpot or slow cooker, put it in a big pot on the stove and simmer for at least 4 hours over low heat. Read on for a vegetarian option.

Ingredients

- 1 pound of ground beef
- 1 chopped onion
- 1 tsp of minced garlic
- ½ bell pepper, diced
- 3 cups of cooked beans (black, kidney, pinto)
- 1 can of diced tomatoes
- 3 tbsp of chili powder
- 1 tbsp of cumin powder
- 1 cup of broth or water

Directions

1. Add all the ingredients into the crockpot and stir will to combine. (You do not need to cook the ground beef ahead of time.)
2. Cook on low for 8 hours.
3. Can you believe that's it?

Vegetarian Chili

Ingredients

- 1 chopped onion
- 1 tsp of minced garlic
- ½ bell pepper, diced
- 3 cups of cooked beans (black, kidney, pinto)
- 1 can of corn, drained or 2 cups of frozen corn
- 1 can of diced tomatoes
- 3 tbsp of chili powder
- 1 tbsp of cumin powder
- 1 cup of broth or water

Directions

4. Add all the ingredients into the crockpot and stir will to combine.
5. Cook on low for 8 hours.
6. Your tasty vegetarian chili is ready!

Wondering what to do with your leftover chili? Here are some tasty ideas.

Chili Pie

Ingredients

- 2 cups of Leftover Chili
- 2 cups of cooked rice
- 1 batch of cornbread batter
- Can of chilis and onions, drained

Directions

1. Stir rice into the leftover chili, then spread it into a seasoned cast iron skillet.
2. In a bowl, prepare cornbread batter with the recipe from the Scratch Basics chapter.
3. Then stir in well-drained chilis and onions.
4. Spread the batter over your skillet of chili mixture.
5. Bake at 350 for 30 minutes or until the cornbread batter is fully cooked.

Chili Mac

Here's another way to extend that chili. If you don't eat boxed macaroni and cheese, you can use plain macaroni and top your chili mac with some shredded cheddar.

Ingredients

- 1 box of macaroni and cheese
- Leftover chili

Directions

1. Prepared the macaroni and cheese according to the instructions on the box.
2. Stir in your leftover chili.
3. Put a lid on the pot and heat the mixture thoroughly, stirring often.
4. Serve when the mixture is piping hot.

Baked Beans

You can serve this as a side dish or the main dish.

Ingredients

- 1 piece of country ham with juices OR 2 pieces of uncooked bacon
- 1 tsp of cooking oil

- 4 cups of cooked of navy beans
- 1 can of crushed tomatoes
- 1 tbsp of onion powder
- 1 tsp of garlic powder
- 1 tsp of dry mustard
- ¼ cup of brown sugar or (optional) molasses
- 1 tbsp of white vinegar
- Salt and Pepper to taste

Directions

- Dice the ham or bacon into bite-sized pieces, then fry it lightly in the cooking oil in an ovenproof pan. (But not cast iron, as you will be using tomato products.)
- Add the beans, crushed tomatoes, water, molasses or sugar, mustard, vinegar, salt, and pepper.
- Put this in the oven at 350 for 30-45 minutes or until heated through.

Thrifty Dinners

With these recipes, you WILL have leftovers. I recommend serving food in the kitchen instead of sitting it on the table. It makes it take a little more effort to grab seconds (and thirds), so you generally will have a bit more food left over.

If you serve bread on the side, it will make the meals even more filling.

Roasted Chicken

This is a very simple meal, but classic and delicious enough to serve to guests. When times are tight, I like to dish out the meat in the kitchen onto individual plates and place the sides on the table for seconds.

Ingredients:

- 5-6 pound whole chicken
- 1 medium onion, peeled and cut in half
- 1 head of garlic
- Salt, pepper, and herbs to taste

- Potatoes and carrots, chopped up

Directions:

1. Preheat your oven to 425.
2. Rinse the chicken, inside and out under running water. (Be sure to wash out your sink with a bleach solution afterwards to keep your kitchen free of bacteria that could cause foodborne illness.)
3. If there is a package of "giblets and guts" inside your chicken, remove it. You can use this later for gravy, add it to your homemade stock, or cook it up for the pets. Keep in mind that liver will give an off-flavor to your stock.
4. Insert the entire head of garlic into the cavity of the chicken. You don't have to peel the garlic first – just put the entire head in there for a rich, garlic-flavored meat.
5. Cut the onion in half and place it, cut side down, in the roasting pan. This will keep the chicken raised up out of the drippings. If you are using a

roasting pan with a rack, you can put the onion in the cavity with the garlic.

6. Sprinkle the chicken liberally with salt, pepper, and herbs.
7. Place your vegetables around the chicken.
8. Place this in the oven, uncovered for about an hour and a half. Using a meat thermometer in the thickest part of the breast, check to see if it is done. The temperature should be 180 degrees Fahrenheit. If you don't have a meat thermometer, gently give the leg a twist. When the chicken is completely cooked, the leg should separate very easily under the lightest pressure.
9. Remove the chicken from the roasting pan and allow it to rest for 15 minutes at room temperature.
10. Carve the chicken, discarding the garlic and onion from the cavity. Put aside the skin for use in your broth, later.

Be sure to make gravy from the drippings. See the Scratch Cooking chapter for instructions.

Chicken broth

Don't throw out that chicken carcass! You can get more bang for your poultry buck by making broth with it. Use this same process for turkey broth.

1. After dinner, remove most of the meat from the bones and place it in the refrigerator. You'll be left with a rather desolate-looking carcass.
2. Put that in your crockpot along with the reserved skin, neck, and giblets (if you didn't use those for gravy). Add some veggies like carrots, peppers, and celery. Add a couple of tablespoons of salt, a head of garlic and 4-6 onions. Note: there's no need to peel the vegetables as long as they are organic - just wash them well.)
3. Fill the crockpot with water and add your favorite spices (not sage, if you intend to preserve the broth - it tastes terrible when canned or frozen). I like to use whole peppercorns, salt, oregano, and bay leaves.

4. Put the crockpot on low for 12-14 hours and let it simmer undisturbed overnight.

5. The next day, strain the contents of the crockpot into a large container - I use a big soup pot and a metal colander.

6. After allowing the bones to cool remove any meat that you would like to add to your soup. Take all of the meat that you put in the refrigerator the night before and cut it into bite-sized pieces. I like a mixture of light meat and dark meat for this purpose. Also cut up the meat you removed from the crockpot.

Freezing the broth

1. Allow your broth to cool completely. Use a heavy-duty freezer bag (I like the kind with the actual zipper.)

2. If you are adding poultry to the broth, place the desired amount in the bottom of the freezer bag. If you aren't adding the poultry, skip this step.

3. Ladle the cooled broth into the bag, leaving 2 inches of headspace at the top.
4. Seal the bag securely, then lay it flat on a cookie sheet. Repeat this process until all of the broth is bagged up.
5. Freeze the broth flat overnight. After that, it should be frozen solid. Label the bags with a Sharpie, including the date. The flat bags of broth can be stacked in the freezer for about 6 months.

Leftover Fried Rice

This is a great way to extend a single serving of meat to provide dinner for an entire family. Feel free to get creative and use other types of meat and additional veggies. If the vegetables are pre-cooked, add them at the very end, giving them just enough time in the skillet to get warmed up.

Ingredients:

- 1 cup of cooked chicken (or other meat), cut into bite-sized pieces

- ½ cup to 1 cup of cooked rice per person
- 1 small onion, minced
- 2 cloves of garlic, minced
- ¼ cup of shredded carrot
- 1-2 eggs (Use 1 egg per 2 cups of rice, not to exceed two eggs.)
- 1 cup of frozen green peas
- 2 tbsp of soy sauce
- 1 tsp of powdered ginger
- 1 tbsp of cooking oil

Directions:

1. In a large skillet or wok, heat cooking oil over a medium heat.
2. Crack eggs and mix them in a bowl with a whisk. Reserve them for later in the cooking process.
3. Add garlic, onion, and meat.
4. Stir fry for a few minutes until everything is lightly golden.
5. Add carrots and stir fry for another minute or two.
6. Add eggs and let them cook for 1 minute without stirring so they get a little bit firm. Then, stir constantly for a couple of minutes so that they

break up as they're cooking, leaving only tiny pieces of egg throughout the mixture of ingredients.

7. Sprinkle with ginger powder, then stir in soy sauce.
8. Increase heat to high, then stir in rice and peas.
9. Stirring constantly, cook until everything is heated through.

Serve topped with chopped green onion and optional dried crushed chili peppers.

Noodles with Peanut Sauce

Ingredients:

- 1 pack of spaghetti, cooked
- 1/3 cup of peanut butter (smooth or crunchy)
- ½ cup of broth or water
- 1 tbsp of soy sauce
- 1 tbsp of rice vinegar
- 1 tbsp of garlic powder
- 1 tsp of cumin
- 1 tsp of ginger powder
- 1 tsp of sugar or honey
- 1 bag of frozen green beans

- Optional: Crushed red chili pepper flakes

Directions:

1. Cook your noodles until they're al dente. During the last minute of cooking, add your frozen green beans.
2. Drain the pasta and beans.
3. In a large skillet, add peanut butter, soy sauce, rice vinegar, garlic powder, ginger powder, cumin, and broth or water.
4. Warm this up on low heat and whisk constantly.
5. When the sauce is smooth and creamy, add the sugar or honey and whisk for another minute.
6. Remove from heat.
7. Stir in the drained pasta and beans until everything is covered with the peanut sauce. Sprinkle with chili peppers if desired.

Chicken Cacciatore

Ingredients

- 2-3 pounds of chicken thighs
- 1 28-ounce can of diced tomatoes
- 1 can of mushrooms
- 1 bell pepper, diced
- 1 onion, diced
- 1 tsp each of basil, oregano, and thyme

Directions

1. Preheat the oven to 325.
2. Place everything but the chicken in an oven-safe casserole dish. Stir it well to combine.
3. Add the chicken thighs.
4. Cover the dish tightly with tin foil.
5. Bake for one hour or until chicken is falling apart.

Serve over rice, potatoes, or pasta.

Crockpot Roast Dinner

Ingredients:

- Pork or beef roast (plan on 1 pound per person so you have leftovers and don't be afraid to go with a cheap cut of meat)
- 1 large onion
- 1 potato per person
- 2 carrots per person
- 2 cloves of garlic, whole
- ½ cup of water
- 1/2 cup of another liquid, which can be one or a combination of these ingredients: water, beef broth, red wine, apple juice (for pork), cola, strong unsweetened coffee)
- Salt and pepper to taste
- 2 tbsp of flour and 2 tbsp of butter for making gravy

Directions:

1. Cut an onion in half and lay it, flat side down, in the bottom of a slow cooker (crock pot).

2. Cut the carrots and potatoes into bite sized chunks and add them to the bottom of the crockpot.
3. Place your roast on top of the vegetables, then add the garlic cloves to the top of the roast.
4. Season the roast with salt and pepper.
5. Pour the liquid on top of the roast.
6. Put the lid on the crockpot and cook this on low for 8-10 hours. The long cooking time means that you can go with a lower quality cut of meat and it will still be fork-tender.
7. At serving time, melt butter in the bottom of a skillet on the stove top. Once the butter is melted, quickly whisk in 2 tbsp of flour until you have a white creamy concoction with no lumps.
8. Ladle out 1 ½ cups of the liquid from the crockpot and pour it into the skillet.
9. Using your whisk, incorporate the flour and butter mixture with the liquid. Reduce the heat to low and allow this mixture to gently simmer

while you get the meat and vegetables ready to serve. You may need to thin the gravy with an additional half cup of water.

10. Remove the meat and vegetables from the slow cooker, reserving the remaining liquid for your future stew.

11. Slice the meat, reserving a third of it for stew. (If you put all of the meat out, chances are you won't have leftovers, because this is melt-in-your-mouth good.)

Serve meat and vegetables with gravy.

Leftover Roast Stew

Ingredients:

- Leftovers from Crockpot Roast Dinner
- Water or broth

Directions:

Most of the prep for this stew is done when you are putting away your leftovers. Stirring in the additional liquid before you put this in the refrigerator will allow the flavors to meld until you are ready to make your stew.

1. In a large storage container, stir 1-2 cups of water or broth into your reserved cooking liquid. If you have leftover gravy, stir that in, too.
2. Cut the rest of your roast into bite sized pieces, then add it to the liquid.
3. Add any leftover vegetables to the meat and liquid.
4. Add 1 can of mixed vegetables, including liquid.
5. Put this in the refrigerator for 1-2 days.
6. Heat on the stove top at a simmer for 20 minutes. You can serve this with crusty bread. If there isn't quite enough for a family meal, serve it over wide noodles or rice for a filling, hearty dinner.

Pantry Spaghetti Sauce

If you don't have some of these spices and ingredients, don't worry – go ahead and make it! This recipe is very forgiving!

Ingredients:

- 1 can of crushed tomatoes
- 3 cloves of garlic

- 1 medium onion
- 1 tbsp of sugar
- 1 tsp of salt
- 1 tsp of thyme
- 1 tsp of oregano
- 1 tbsp of basil
- black pepper to taste
- 1 pinch of paprika
- 2 tbsp of olive oil
- Optional: ½ cup of diced bell pepper
- Optional: ½ cup of fresh sliced mushrooms or 1 small can of drained mushrooms
- Optional: 1 pound of ground beef
- Fresh grated Parmesan for the top

Directions:

1. In a food processor, place a small amount of the crushed tomatoes, garlic, onion, spices, sugar, and optional bell peppers if you're using them. Process until pureed.
2. Pour the rest of the crushed tomatoes, the pureed mixture and the optional mushrooms into a stockpot.

3. If you want to add meat, stir in your uncooked ground meat or meatballs now too.
4. Simmer on a low heat for about 3 hours. (You can cook it for longer if you want to, or you can cook this all day on low in the crock pot.) Drizzle with olive oil and allow it to cook for another 15 minutes.
5. Serve over pasta, topped with Parmesan.

Cheapo Chicken and Dumplings

Ingredients

- 2 one-quart cartons of chicken broth
- 1 can of chicken
- 1 tsp each of poultry seasoning, garlic powder, and onion powder

Dumplings

- 2 cups of flour
- Extra flour for dusting the counter and the rolling pin
- 1 egg

- 1 cup of water
- Salt, pepper, and parsley to taste

Directions

1. In a large stockpot, combine broth, chicken, and poultry seasoning. Bring this to a simmer while you make your dumplings.
2. In a large mixing bowl, combine flour and seasonings. Stir in water and egg, combining well. You will have a dry crumbly mixture.
3. Squeeze the dough by handfuls and put it on a counter that has been dusted with flour.
4. Roll out the dough until it is flat, about ¼ inch thick.
5. Using a pizza cutter or a sharp knife, cut the dough into strips or squares, according to your preference. Allow it to dry on the counter for up to 2 hours.
6. Press each dumpling with a fork, then drop it carefully into the simmering soup.

7. Allow this to cook for 10 minutes or until the dumplings have floated to the top. Serve immediately.

Serving Suggestions

Add a can of cream of chicken soup or one cup of white sauce and a can of drained peas and carrots to make this a heartier meal.

Taco Pie

Ingredients

- 4 large soft tortillas
- 2 cups of refried beans
- ½ cup of shredded cheddar cheese
- 1 cup of drained diced tomatoes
- ½ cup of diced onion
- 2 tbsp of parsley
- Optional: ½ cup of diced bell or jalapeno peppers
- Optional: sour cream

Directions

1. Grease the bottom of a cast-iron skillet and then lay the first soft tortilla on it.
2. Mix the tomatoes, onions, parsley, and optional peppers to make a quick salsa.
3. Spread a layer of refried beans on the tortilla then top that with salsa, then cheese.
4. Repeat the layers until you get to the top tortilla. Spread a small amount of salsa on top. Cover it with tin foil, taking care not to touch the top tortilla with the foil.
5. Bake at 350 for 20 minutes or until it's heated through. If you have cheese remaining, add it to the top and put it back in the oven until the cheese is melted and bubbly.

6. Slice it in quarters like a pie and serve with sour cream.

Casseroles and Concoctions

I know, I know. Casseroles sound very "50s Housewife." But when you're on a budget, casseroles are a great way to make a little bit of food stretch further in a tasty way.

The Casserole Formula

And, to make it even better, there's a formula. This is loosely based on Amy Dacyczyn's Universal Casserole recipe from *The Complete Tightwad Gazette*. (That's a book I highly recommend for everyone trying to live a more frugal lifestyle.)

- 1 cup of protein
- 1-2 cups of veggies
- 1-2 cups of carbs
- 1 1/2 cups of sauce
- Spices
- Topping

It's honestly that easy.

Your protein might be leftover meat, a can of tuna, ground meat, or beans. Your veggie can be any tasty thing you have that will go well with the meat. We often use either frozen or canned green peas, green beans, cauliflower, broccoli, or mixed vegetables.

Your carbs can be pasta, rice, potatoes, or whatever grain you have kicking around in abundance.

Your sauce is the "glue" that holds the whole thing together. It might be white sauce, gravy, a can of condensed cream of whatever soup, tomato sauce, or cheese sauce.

Casseroles are pretty yummy when they have some kind of tasty, crispy topping. This might be bread crumbs and butter, cracker crumbs and butter, shredded cheese, those little cans of French-fried onions – whatever tasty thing you have on hand.

Season it with whatever spices you have that are appropriate – Italian seasonings, garlic salt, chili powder – whatever you think sounds good with your concoction.

To make your casserole, combine your cooked meat, your frozen or canned veggies, your cooked carbs, your spices, and your sauce.

Bake at 350 for 30-45 minutes, or until your sauce is bubbling. Then add your topping and bake it for another 5-10 minutes until it is crispy.

Tuna (or Chicken) Noodle Casserole

Tuna casserole is a love-it-or-hate-it kind of thing. When my kids were younger, they loved it. As they got older, they didn't love it so much. However, this is a thrifty and simple dish to make.

Tuna is cheaper but if you double-HATE tuna, make this recipe with canned chicken.

- 1 can of condensed cream of mushroom soup OR 1 cup of white sauce
- 1 cup of milk
- 2 cans of tuna, drained (or chicken)

- 3-4 cups of noodles, cooked (I like wide egg noodles for this, but any kind of pasta will do)
- 1 bag of frozen green peas
- ½ tsp of garlic salt
- ½ tsp of onion powder
- Black pepper to taste
- ½ cup of shredded cheddar cheese
- ½ cup of bread crumbs

Directions

Preheat oven to 375.

1. In a greased baking dish, combine the soup or white sauce with milk, mixing well.
2. Stir in the noodles, tuna or chicken, and peas.
3. Season with garlic salt, black pepper, and onion powder.
4. Bake at 375 for 30 minutes.
5. Meanwhile, combine the shredded cheese and breadcrumbs in a bowl.

6. Top your casserole with the cheese and breadcrumb mixture and return it to the oven for 5 more minutes.

Spaghetti Pie

This is a great way to make the most of your spaghetti dinner leftovers. Alternatively, you can use a jar of marinara sauce and no meat.

Ingredients:

- Leftover spaghetti with meat sauce OR a jar of marinara sauce
- 1 serving of cooked pasta for each family member
- 1-2 eggs
- 1 cup of cottage cheese
- ¼ cup of Parmesan cheese, plus additional for the top
- 1 tsp of garlic powder
- ½ cup of toasted bread crumbs
- Optional: extra chopped vegetables like tomato, mushroom, bell pepper, spinach, and onion

Directions:

1. Preheat the oven to 350 degrees Fahrenheit.
2. In a large bowl, beat the eggs and cottage cheese with garlic powder and Parmesan cheese. Alternatively, you can also blend this together in a food processor.
3. Stir in cooked pasta until it is well coated.
4. Stir in leftover spaghetti sauce and optional chopped vegetables.
5. Pour the mixture into a greased oven-proof pie plate or skillet. (I use my cast-iron frying pan for this.)
6. Cover with foil and bake for 30 minutes in your preheated oven.
7. Mix extra Parmesan and toasted breadcrumbs for the topping.
8. Increase heat to 425 degrees Fahrenheit. Remove foil, top with additional Parmesan and toasted breadcrumbs, and bake for an additional 15 minutes, until the top is lightly crisped.

9. Remove the pie from the oven and allow it to set for 15 minutes before slicing.

Chicken & Broccoli Casserole

Ingredients

- 2 cups of leftover chicken, cut into bite-sized pieces
- 2 cups frozen broccoli
- 1 can cream of chicken/mushroom soup or 1 cup of white sauce
- 2 cups of cooked rice
- 1 cup of shredded cheddar cheese
- ½ cup of mayo
- ½ cup breadcrumbs
- 2 tbsp of melted butter

Directions

1. Preheat the oven to 350.
2. Add all the ingredients but the breadcrumbs and butter to a greased baking dish and combine well.

3. Top the casserole with breadcrumbs, then drizzle melted butter on top.
4. Bake for 30 minutes or until it's heated through and the topping is golden brown.

Cheeseburger Casserole

Ingredients

- 1 pound of ground beef
- 1 tbsp of minced garlic
- ½ an onion, minced
- 1 package of macaroni
- 2 can of tomato soup
- 1 cup of white sauce OR 1 can of cream of mushroom soup
- Salt and pepper to taste
- 1 cup shredded cheddar cheese
- 1 tube of crescent rolls (or your own biscuit dough)
- Butter as needed
- Optional: ¼ cup diced dill pickles
- Optional: 2 slices of bacon, cooked crisp

Directions

1. In a skillet, cook the ground beef with onion and garlic.
2. At the same time, cook the macaroni in a pot and preheat the oven to 375 degrees.
3. When the ground beef is browned, stir in both cans of soup and remove it from the heat.
4. In a greased casserole dish, stir together the soup and meat mixture, the macaroni, and the bacon and pickles if you're using them.
5. Top it with the shredded cheese.
6. Spread the crescent roll dough on top of the casserole. Brush it with butter.
7. Bake the casserole at 375 for 30 minutes or until the dough is golden brown.

Deep Dish Pizza Casserole

This is a cheap and thrifty knock-off of Chicago-style pizza.

Ingredients

- 1 tube of refrigerated biscuits
- 1 cup of shredded mozzarella cheese
- 2 cups of pizza toppings: Cooked ground beef, cooked Italian sausage, pepperoni, diced bell peppers, chopped onion, sliced mushrooms, etc.
- 1 28-ounce can of spaghetti sauce OR 3 and ½ cups of homemade sauce
- 2 tbsp of Italian seasoning
- ½ cup of Parmesan cheese

Directions

1. Preheat your oven to 375
2. Grease casserole dish really well – you don't want this to stick.
3. Open your tube of biscuit dough. Roll the biscuits out to create a pizza crust
4. Then lay it in the casserole dish. The dough needs to go all the way up the sides of the dish.
5. Sprinkle half of your mozzarella cheese on the dough.

6. Top the dough with your favorite pizza toppings.
7. Spread your spaghetti sauce evenly over the pizza, then sprinkle with Italian seasonings, the rest of the mozzarella, and the Parmesan cheese.
8. Bake your delish pizza for 45 minutes to an hour, or until the dough is cooked through.
9. Delete the number of your local takeout pizza joint from your phone.

If you have leftovers

This reheats far better in the oven than in in the microwave.

Scalloped Potato and Ham Casserole

Ingredients:

- 6 cups of dehydrated of thinly sliced potatoes
- 2 cups of milk
- 2 tbsp of flour or cornstarch
- 1 thinly sliced onion
- 1 tsp of garlic powder
- 1 tsp of nutmeg
- 1 tbsp of thyme
- 1 tbsp of parsley
- Salt and pepper to taste
- 1 slice of vacuum-packed, shelf stable country ham

Directions:

1. Grease a baking dish and preheat your oven to 350.
2. In a bowl, combine water, powdered milk, flour, and spices.

3. Open your package of country ham and pour any liquid into the bowl.
4. Chop the ham into bite-sized pieces.
5. Layer potatoes, ham, and onion slices.
6. Whisk together the contents of your bowl, then pour it over the contents of your baking dish.
7. Bake at 350 for 45 minutes. Let it rest for 5 minutes.

Lasagna Casserole

This is lasagna with a little less fuss. It's absolutely delicious with or without the ground beef, so if your budget is tight, don't hesitate to skip the meat.

You can use other types of hearty pasta like ziti or rotini if you don't have lasagna noodles on hand.

Ingredients

- 1 package of lasagna noodles

- Olive oil
- OPTIONAL INGREDIENTS: 1 pound of cooked ground beef (you can leave this out for a vegetarian dish) and/or 1 bag of frozen spinach
- 1 large onion, chopped
- 1 can of canned mushrooms, drained
- 2 tbsp of minced garlic
- 1 28-ounce can of spaghetti sauce (or 3.5 cups of homemade sauce)
- 1 cup of shredded mozzarella cheese
- 1 cup of cottage cheese
- 1 egg
- ¼ cup of Parmesan

Directions

1. Break up the Lasagna noodles into about 8 pieces per noodle.
2. Cook the noodles until they're firm but tender (al dente.)
3. In a skillet, brown the beef (if you're using it), garlic, onions, and mushrooms. If you aren't using beef, stir in the bag of spinach once the

garlic, mushrooms, and onions are cooked.

4. When the meat and veggies are cooked, stir in the spaghetti sauce.
5. In a food processor, whip together the cottage cheese, egg, and Parmesan cheese.
6. Grease a large casserole dish and preheat the oven to 375.
7. Put a layer of spaghetti sauce on the casserole dish. Top it with a layer of the cottage cheese mixture and a layer of the cooked noodles. Repeat until you've used up everything, finishing with a layer of sauce.
8. Top the final layer with the mozzarella cheese.
9. Bake for 25 minutes or until the casserole is bubbly and the cheese is golden brown.

Breakfast for Dinner

Who doesn't love breakfast for dinner? It's quick, easy, thrifty, and delicious. Plus, kids usually feel like they're really getting away with something, which makes it a lot more fun.

Scrambled eggs, cereal, and toast are all tasty and easy. Here are a couple more frugalicious recipes to add to your repertoire.

Pancakes

The great thing about pancakes is that you can top them with whatever you happen to have kicking around. After the basic pancake recipe, you'll find some ideas for toppings and add ins.

Ingredients

- 1 cup milk
- 1 egg
- 2 tbsp vegetable oil, plus more for cooking
- 1 cup of flour
- 2 tbsp of sugar
- 1 tsp of baking powder

- 1/4 tsp of salt

Directions

1. Combine all of the dry ingredients in a bowl with a whisk.
2. Add the wet ingredients mix everything thoroughly. Don't worry if there are a few small lumps.
3. Let the batter sit for 10-15 minutes
4. Heat up a skillet with a little bit of oil for cooking the pancakes.
5. The skillet is hot enough when water sprinkled onto it sizzles and bubbles.
6. Plop about 2 tablespoons of batter into the skillet – you can cook 3-4 of these at a time.
7. Cook for 3 minutes or until you see lots of bubbles on the surface of the pancake.
8. Flip them and cook for a couple more minutes, then place the finished pancakes on a platter in a 200-degree oven.
9. Add more oil and cook more pancakes until they're all done.

Rainbow pancakes: If you happen to have any sprinkles kicking around from birthdays past, stir some into your pancake batter. They'll melt into a cool tie die pattern. This is what I always used to serve at slumber party breakfasts.

Fruity pancakes: Stir 1 cup of frozen fruit into the batter. (Chop up the fruit if it's bigger than bite-sized. Then make a fruit syrup on the stovetop. To make the syrup, bring 1 cup of water, ½ cup of sugar, and 1 cup of fruit to a boil. Cook until the fruit begins to get soft and the syrup begins to thicken a little bit.

Cinnamon roll pancakes. Stir 1 tbsp of cinnamon and 1/3 cup of brown sugar into the pancake batter. Then, make icing with 1 cup of cream cheese and 1 cup of powdered sugar. Spread the icing on the pancakes and add a light dusting of cinnamon to the top.

Biscuits and Gravy

This is a flexible recipe straight from the South. Use the biscuit recipe in the Scratch Basics chapter or use any bread you happen to have that might be a little bit stale as the basis for this incredibly frugal dish.

- 1 slice of ham, 2 slices of bacon, or 3 sausages
- Cooking oil
- 2 cups of milk
- ¼ cup of flour
- Salt and pepper to taste

Directions:

1. Heat cooking oil in a skillet on the stove.
2. Add your choice of breakfast meat, then fry on a low heat.
3. Use a slotted spoon to remove the meat when you've browned it lightly and rendered some of the fat from it into the skillet.

4. Chop up the meat to add to the gravy later.
5. Sprinkle the bubbling fat with the flour and quickly whisk it to get rid of any lumps. Allow the flour to brown lightly.
6. Pour in half the milk and season with salt and pepper. Whisk constantly for a few minutes until the mixture is very thick.
7. Whisk in the rest of the milk and reduce the heat. Add your chopped meat.
8. Allow the gravy to thicken to the desired consistency. If it's too thick, add water. If it's not thick enough, remove a little bit of the liquid and mix in some more flour before re-adding it.

Serve immediately over biscuits or bread to feed a whole family something filling from a single serving of meat.

Oatmeal

I prefer rolled oats to start you off if you
don't generally make oatmeal from scratch.
Old-fashioned oats have been steamed and
then rolled. They are sometimes labeled
"rolled oats" and sometimes "old-fashioned
oats."

Ingredients

- ½ cup of oats
- 1 cup of water (or milk)
- A pinch of salt

Directions

1. Bring 1 cup water or milk and salt (if
   desired) to a boil in a small saucepan.
2. Stir in 1/2 cup oats and reduce heat
   to medium.
3. Cook the oats, stirring occasionally,
   for 5 minutes.
4. Remove from the heat, cover and let
   stand for 2 to 3 minutes.

Oatmeal is all about the toppings. You can add fruit (canned or frozen), jam, maple syrup, nuts, honey – the only limit is your pantry. I found that when my kids got to dress up their oatmeal, they were a lot more jazzed about eating it.

Muffins

This is a basic muffin recipe. You can add in whatever goodies you like to personalize them.

Ingredients

- 2 cups of flour
- 1 tbsp of baking powder
- 1/2 tsp of salt
- ½ cup sugar
- 1 egg, beaten
- 1 cup milk
- 1/4 cup melted butter, shortening, or coconut oil

Directions

1. Preheat the oven to 375
2. Grease your muffin pans.

3. Mix the flour, baking powder, salt, and sugar in a large bowl.
4. Add the egg, milk, and butter and stir it just a teeny bit – it should still be lumpy.
5. Add your goodies.
6. Dip your muffin batter into your muffin tin, filling each cup 2/3 full.
7. Bake for about 20 to 25 or until a toothpick inserted into a muffin comes out clean and dry.

Goodies

- Add in any of the following goodies:
- Drained canned fruit
- Frozen fruit chopped into little pieces
- Chocolate chips
- Nuts
- Raisins or other dried fruit
- Cinnamon, nutmeg, and/or allspice

Banana Bread

This is a fantastic way to salvage almost-trash bananas. I even buy them when they're on last day of sale for the very purpose of banana bread.

Ingredients

- 4 very ripe bananas
- 1/2 cup of melted butter or coconut oil
- 3/4 cup of sugar
- 2 eggs
- 1 tsp vanilla extract
- 1½ cups of flour
- 1 tsp baking soda
- A pinch of salt

Directions

1. Preheat oven to 350.
2. Place bananas in a large bowl and mash them with a potato masher.
3. Add the other ingredients and then stir until everything is just combined.
4. Pour the batter into a greased loaf pan and bake for 50-60 minutes, or until a toothpick inserted into the center of the loaf comes out clean.

5. Let it cool in the pan for 15 minutes, then tip it out onto a cutting board.
6. Serve with butter.

Breakfast Cookies

This recipe is oh-so-versatile, and you can use up whatever you have on hand.

Ingredients

- 1/2 cup of sugar (brown or white)
- 3/4 cups of applesauce
- 1 cup of flour
- 2 tsp of baking powder
- 1/2 tsp of salt
- 1 tsp of cinnamon
- 1/4 tsp of allspice
- 1/8 tsp of powdered cloves
- 1 cup of rolled oats

Now the creative part - from one cup to up to a cup and a half (total) of "whatever" –

I've offered some suggestions, but basically anything you have on hand that sounds like it would be yummy:

- sunflower seeds
- walnuts
- pecans
- raisins
- dried cranberries
- white chocolate chips
- flax seeds
- butterscotch chips
- pumpkin seeds
- wheat germ
- granola
-
- dry cereal

Directions:

1. Preheat the oven to 350F
2. In a large mixing bowl, stir together sugar and applesauce.
3. Sift flour, baking powder and salt together then stir into the applesauce mixture.
4. Stir in your other assorted ingredients until the batter is just combined.
5. Drop large spoonfuls of batter onto a greased cookie sheet - they don't

really spread much and get bigger, so
they will remain approximately the
same size.
6. Bake for 10 minutes.
7. Allow them to cool on the cookie
   sheet for 10 minutes, then move
   them to a plate to cool further.

Souper Duper Suppers

A lot of folks think those Depression Era techniques for stretching food are only for a worst case, SHTF scenario. But in truth, those ideas are good for every day, because the price of food just keeps going up, up, UP. It's more important now than ever to make your food go further.

The ability to make the food you have feed more people (and leave them feeling full and satisfied) will stand you in good stead if things go horribly wrong. But I think it's important to do this in the meantime too. If we went back to the ways that our grandmothers made food last during the Great Depression, we could take a big chunk out of our grocery bills, eat more scratch cooking, and stop wasting so much food.

There is nothing like a pot of soup. It makes the house smell comforting and enticing as it simmers on the stove (or in the crockpot).

It's a delicious and warming meal. But even that isn't the very best thing about soup. The best thing about soup is that you can feed a LOT of people a hot, satisfying meal for just a LITTLE bit of money.

When I lived in Canada, some nights we had lots of people show up for dinner. On those evenings, I'd add an extra potato for each extra person I hadn't been expecting. Add a loaf of homemade bread, and I had dinner on the table for however many folks we were feeding.

Here's another good thing about soup. When I don't have quite enough leftovers to make 2 full servings for my youngest daughter and me, but it's a bit more than one serving, I often make soup. I can broth on a regular basis, so it's an easy thing to grab a jar of broth, chop up the meat and add some vegetables and a grain. You can stretch your soup by adding barley, pasta, or rice.

If you have some bread to serve with it and a little sprinkle of parmesan or cheddar for the top, you have a hot, comforting meal for pennies.

Cabbage Roll Soup

Ingredients

- 1 pound of ground beef
- 1 large onion, chopped
- 5 cups packed chopped cabbage
- 2 tbsp of minced garlic
- 1 28-ounce can of crushed tomatoes
- 1 28-ounce can of diced tomatoes
- 2 tbsp of brown sugar
- ¼ cup of white vinegar
- 1 tbsp of oregano
- 1 tbsp of basil
- 1 cup of uncooked rice
- Salt and pepper to taste

Directions

1. In a skillet, cook the ground beef, onion, and garlic together.
2. Season with salt and pepper.

3. In a crockpot, combine the tomatoes, sugar, vinegar, spices and rice. Then stir in the meat mixture.
4. Finally, add the chopped cabbage.
5. Cook on low for at least 8 hours.

Pantry Vegetable Soup

This recipe is very versatile. If you are missing any of the ingredients, it's fine – just use what you have on hand. If you have frozen vegetables instead of canned, that will work too. And of course, you can also substitute fresh ingredients for canned but you will require more cooking time for the potatoes.

Ingredients:

- 1 large (46 oz) can of tomato juice
- 1 can each of potatoes, corn, green beans, peas, and carrots
- 2 cups of cooked beans (navy, pinto, white, kidney - you pick)
- 1 tbsp each of thyme, basil, and oregano

- 1 tbsp of garlic powder
- 1 tbsp of onion powder
- 1 tsp of paprika
- 1 cup of macaroni or other short pasta
- Salt and pepper to taste

Directions

1. Pour all the cans, undrained, into a large stockpot.
2. Stir in the seasonings.
3. Bring it to a boil then reduce it to a simmer for 15 minutes.
4. Add the pasta and cook it for another 10 minutes or until the pasta is fully cooked.

Serving Suggestions

Serve with fry bread.

Loaded Potato Soup

You can also use leftover potatoes for this soup if you have enough for everyone.

Ingredients:

- 1-2 potatoes per person
- 1 diced onion
- 1 cup of milk
- 2 cups of water
1. Optional toppings: homemade yogurt or sour cream, shredded cheese, fried onions, bacon, and/or chives.

Directions:

2. Cook the potatoes in boiling water, then drain them.
3. Use a potato masher to break up the potatoes well. If you want, you can run the entire batch through the food processor, but my family prefers the chunks of potatoes.
4. In a large stockpot, stir the potatoes, onions, milk, and water together
5. Heat this up, bringing it to a simmer. If it's too thick, you can add more

milk or water. (Milk will make it richer, but if your supplies are limited, water will be fine.)

6. Top the soup like you would a baked potato, with homemade yogurt or sour cream, shredded cheese, fried onions, bacon, and/or chives.

Split Pea Soup

If you have some salt pork, ham, or bacon, you can add that into your soup for a different flavor.

Ingredients

- 1 pound of split peas, rinsed and sorted
- 2 quarts (8 cups) of water
- 1 diced onion
- 1 cup of diced carrot
- 1 tsp of celery seed
- Black pepper to taste
- Salt and pepper to taste

Directions

1. In a large stockpot, bring peas, spices, and water to a boil.
2. Reduce heat to a simmer and then cook the soup for 90 minutes.
3. Then add the carrots, cooking for an additional 30 minutes.
4. Use a potato masher or a blender to get the desired consistency for your soup, then ladle it into bowls.
5. Top each serving with some diced ham or crisp fried bacon, if desired.

Creamy Corn Chowder

Ingredients

- 1 can of whole kernel corn
- 1 can of creamed corn
- 1 carton of chicken broth
- ½ cup of milk or cream
- 1 potato, diced
- 1 tbsp of onion powder
- Salt and pepper to taste
- Optional: Parsley

Directions

1. In a stockpot, combine the 2 cans of corn, the broth, potato, and the seasonings.
2. Bring to a simmer for 30 minutes or until the potato is fully cooked.
3. Stir in the milk and heat through.
4. Dish into bowls and sprinkle parsley on top.

Serving Suggestion

Corn chowder can be topped with sour cream and chopped bacon if you have this available.

Tex-Mex Vegetable Soup

This soup is quite versatile and you can throw in any leftover meat you might have on hand for a carnivore version. (It's particularly good with chicken.)

Ingredients

- I 28-ounce can of tomato/vegetable juice
- 2 cups of black beans, cooked

- 1 can of corn
- 3 tbsp of chili powder
- 1 tbsp of cumin
- 2 carrots, diced
- 1 onion, finely chopped
- ½ bell pepper, diced

Directions

1. Add all ingredients to a crockpot.
2. Cook on low for 6 hours or longer.
3. Serve with tortilla chips or cornbread.

Variation

If you have some leftover meat, you can stir it into this soup, but it's very good as a vegetarian dish.

You can grab a single-serving bag of tortilla chips to crumble on top for a little bit of crunch, too.

Lentil Soup

Ingredients

- 2 tbsp of olive oil
- 1 onion, finely chopped

- 2 tbsp minced garlic
- 2 large carrots, diced
- 1 can of diced tomatoes
- 2 cups of dried lentils, any type, rinsed and sorted
- 6 cups of broth or water
- 2 tsp each cumin and turmeric powders
- 1 tsp paprika
- Salt, pepper, and parsley to taste

Directions

1. In a large cooking pot, sauté garlic and onion in the olive oil.
2. Once the veggies are golden and fragrant, add the rest of the ingredients except for the parsley.
3. Bring the soup to a boil, then reduce the heat and simmer it for 45 minutes or until the lentils are tender.
4. Transfer 2 cups of the soup to a food processor and puree it. Add the puree back to the soup and stir well.

Sprinkle parsley on top of each bowl and serve with fry bread.

Some Final Advice

First of all, please remember that this too shall pass. While having financial problems is no walk in the park, you have the power to survive by making changes to the way you deal with money and how you classify needs vs. wants.

Sometimes people like to hide financial problems from their families. They don't want to worry spouses or kids.

But being upfront about what's going on can really help you work together. If your other family members have no idea what's going on, how can they possibly know that they need to change the way they're spending money?

When everyone knows the reality of the situation, they can adjust their expectations about what you've got in the kitchen and what the family can spend money on. But if they have no idea, how can you expect them to behave in alignment with your new budget.

And if you have kids, I strongly urge you to be honest with them. My daughters knew when we were going through hard times. They understood they had to take their lunches, that we couldn't afford to go out to eat, and that we had to stick to a tight budget.

And instead of making them sad and miserable, it taught them many valuable lessons. As they both begin making their ways in the world as young adults now, they've thanked me again and again for the things I taught them about getting by on less. They were so much better prepared for the real world than were some of their classmates who never dealt with hard times.

Of course, only you can decide how you'll handle this situation with your family.

Please know that eventually, things will get better.

They may get better because the situation was short term, or they may get better because you learn to deal with life on less money. But either way, this too shall pass. Life will be brighter one day soon.

Thank you for purchasing this book and helping me to help others.

Love,

Daisy

Shopping List

You don't need to buy everything on this list if you aren't cooking everything in the book. Also – you may already have some of these ingredients stashed away, so don't duplicate items while times are tough.

Protein

- Beans, dried
- Beef, ground
- Chicken thighs
- Chicken, canned
- Chicken, whole
- Country ham
- Eggs
- Lentils
- Roast, pork or beef
- Split peas
- Tuna, canned

Grains

- Cornmeal
- Egg noodles

- Flour
- Flour tortillas
- Lasagna noodles
- Macaroni
- Oats, rolled
- Rice, brown
- Spaghetti

Scratch Basics

- Baking powder
- Baking soda
- Broth
- Brown sugar
- Pepper
- Salt
- Vinegar, white
- White sugar
- Yeast, active dry

Spices

- Allspice
- Basil
- Bay leaf
- Chili powder

- Cinnamon
- Cloves, powdered
- Cumin
- Dry mustard
- Garlic powder
- Hot sauce
- Lemon juice
- Nutmeg
- Onion powder
- Oregano
- Paprika
- Parsley
- Poultry seasoning
- Vanilla extract

Fats

- Butter
- Coconut oil
- Cooking Oil
- Olive oil
- Shortening

Dairy

- Cheese, cheddar

- Cheese, mozzarella
- Cheese, Parmesan
- Milk
- Yogurt (active cultures)

Produce

- Applesauce
- Bananas, ripe
- Bell peppers
- Broccoli, frozen
- Cabbage
- Carrots
- Corn, creamed
- Corn, whole kernel
- Garlic
- Green peas, frozen or canned
- Mushrooms, canned
- Onion
- Potatoes
- Spinach, frozen
- Tomato juice
- Tomatoes, crushed
- Tomatoes, diced

Convenience Items

- Biscuits, refrigerated tube
- Bread crumbs
- Crescent rolls, refrigerated
- Macaroni and cheese, boxed
- Soup, cream of mushroom
- Spaghetti sauce, can or jar
- Tomato soup
- Tortillas, flour

About the Author

Daisy Luther is an author and blogger who lives in the mountains in the Eastern US. For now, anyway. She is the author of *The Prepper's Water Survival Guide* and *The Prepper's Canning Guide*, as well as numerous self-published titles that you can find in her online bookstore on her website.

Her blog is TheOrganicPrepper.com.

Daisy uses her background in alternative journalism to provide a unique perspective on subjects such as current events, preparedness, health, and personal liberty. Daisy's articles are wildly republished throughout alternative media and she has been interviewed and quoted and many mainstream outlets.

She is the coffee-swigging, gun-toting mama of two wonderful, sensible, talented daughters and 4 furry beasts.

Manufactured by Amazon.ca
Bolton, ON

13568806R00081